DUDLEY SCHOOLS LIBRARY
AND INFORMATION SERVICE

KU-337-367

Schools Library and Information Services

S00000687046

Action for the Environment

Transport Solutions

Daniel Gilpin

W
FRANKLIN WATTS
LONDON•SYDNEY

DUDLEY PUBLIC LIBRARIES

L

687046   SCH

J 388

© 2004 Franklin Watts

Franklin Watts
96 Leonard Street
London EC2A 4XD

Franklin Watts Australia
45–51 Huntley Street
Alexandria
NSW 2015

ISBN: 0 7496 5603 4

A CIP catalogue record for this book
is available from the British Library

Printed in Malaysia

Editor: Adrian Cole
Design: Proof Books
Art Director: Jonathan Hair
Picture Research: Kathy Lockley

Acknowledgements

© Airbus, 2004, All rights reserved - Proprietary
Information. Photo by H. Gousse 14 t, 14 b, 15.
Martin Barlow/Art Directors & TRIP Photo Library
29b. Hans Blossey/Still Pictures 2, 11. Martin.
Bond/Still Pictures 13 t. Adrian Cole 16, 31. Vicki
Coombs/Ecoscene 13 b. Stephen Coyne/Ecoscene 22
t. Ron Giling/Still Pictures 5, COVER TL. Richard
Glover/Ecoscene 1, 10. Russell Gordon/Still Pictures
8. © Greenheart Project/Mr Seiichi Kunikata 17 b.
Nick Hawkes/Ecoscene 24. David Hoey/Art Directors
& TRIP Photo Library 25 b. ITDG /Rachel Berger 7.
N.A.S.A./Tom Tschida 26–27. Tony Page/Ecoscene 4,
COVER B. Rex Features 28. Ray Roberts/Ecoscene
COVER TR. Helene Rogers/ Art Directors & TRIP
Photo Library 19 t. J. Sainsbury plc 9. Hartmut
Schwarzbach/Still Pictures 22 b. Copyright © 2001-
2003 Segway LLC 29 t. Ulrich Sonntag/Greenpeace
21. Friedrich Stark/Still Pictures 19 b. Jochen
Tack/Still Pictures 17 t. U.S. DOE Photo 6 t, 12, 18,
20, 23, 25 t, 27 b. Virgin Trains/Milepost 92-1/2 6 b.

Every attempt has been made to clear copyright.
Should there be any inadvertent omission, please
apply to the publisher for rectification.

Contents

World in motion

The transport we use makes up an important part of our lives. But some forms of transport are more harmful to the environment than others. By thinking about the transport we use and how often we use it, we can help to protect the environment around us.

FOSSIL FUEL POLLUTION

Most engines in cars, trains, boats and aeroplanes use petrol or other fossil fuels. These fuels generate energy when they are burned in an engine. Unfortunately, this process also produces carbon dioxide and other polluting 'greenhouse' gases which damage the environment. People are now trying to do more to reduce these emissions.

Cars and other vehicles that use fossil fuels produce high levels of greenhouse gas emissions.

Cyclists in Beijing, China. In busy cities cycling can often be the fastest way to travel short distances.

Action stations

Most forms of transport have a negative effect on the environment, but there are two that have no impact at all. Walking and cycling are completely environmentally friendly. The only energy they use is the energy produced by our own bodies. As well as being good for the environment, walking and cycling are great forms of exercise that can help to keep us healthy.

GLOBAL WARMING

High levels of carbon dioxide are thought to be the main cause of global warming. As the gas builds up in the air (see right) it traps more and more heat from the Sun – like the panes of glass in a greenhouse – warming the Earth's atmosphere and affecting the climate. Most scientists predict that if this continues, more of us will experience extreme weather, such as droughts and storms.

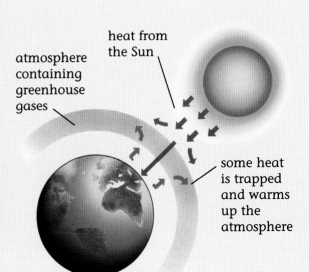

atmosphere containing greenhouse gases

heat from the Sun

some heat is trapped and warms up the atmosphere

Transport networks

The networks on which vehicles travel also affect the environment. Roads, railways and canals help people and goods move around easily. Unfortunately, they often cut through natural habitats and disturb the environment.

Building a new road. The asphalt used to make some roads stops plants growing on them and prevents rainwater reaching the ground.

ROADS AND MOTORWAYS

Roads generally have a bigger impact on the environment than any other transport network. Every year, thousands of people and animals are killed crossing roads. Many anti-road campaigners are trying to encourage people to use other networks, such as railways, and to stop more roads being built, particularly in the developed world.

Railways and canals have a small environmental impact.

RAIL LINKS

Railways have a relatively small impact on the environment because the trains they carry produce less pollution than cars and lorries. Railways usually blend into the environment – their cuttings and verges may actually become havens for wildlife. More cities, such as Kuala Lumpur in Malaysia, are building monorail or 'light railway' networks to help reduce congestion on the roads.

CANALS

In a few places, canals are still used to transport people and goods. The barges that travel on canals move slowly and quietly, and hardly disturb wildlife at all. Many canals actually provide homes for plants, water birds and other animals.

Women in Sri Lanka preparing a new road. Small-scale projects, such as this, improve links to markets and services.

Action stations

Some countries in the developing world have very poor transport networks which increase poverty levels. Many rural roads consist of narrow dirt tracks that prevent people travelling to buy food and collect water. The ITDG has helped local women in Mulberigama, Sri Lanka, to build 1.2 kilometres of gravel road. This small-scale project will have a minimal impact on the environment and will greatly improve people's lives. The road will be used mainly by non-motorised transport, such as bicycles and animal-drawn carts.

Reducing car use

Most families in the developed world have a car, and many have more than one. Although cars can be useful, they are often used far more than is necessary.

These school children in Hong Kong are walking to school. Many people make journeys in cars which could easily be made on foot.

THE SCHOOL RUN

Thousands of parents drive their children to and from school, which saves them time. But these 'school run' journeys are usually only made over short distances. If more children walked or caught the bus to school it would reduce car emissions and cut road congestion.

POPPING TO THE SHOPS

Many people use their cars to go shopping because there is often too much to carry. But driving to the shops to buy one or two things causes unnecessary pollution. Walking or cycling is often just as easy – and much healthier and cheaper, too.

Action stations

A lot of people get into their cars without thinking. Cutting down on unnecessary journeys is one of the easiest ways to reduce pollution and the damage it causes. Many people hope that Internet shopping will change the way people buy goods. Those who have access to the Internet can shop on-line, for example at supermarkets, music retailers and clothing stores, without going anywhere near a car. The goods are then delivered by van, which makes several deliveries in one trip.

Shopping delivered to your door. Services such as this one could cut pollution by reducing the number of journeys people make to the shops.

Driving to work

More people use cars to get to and from work than for any other reason. These journeys often cause congestion and are the main source of pollution in most towns and cities. They are journeys that have to be made, but there are ways to reduce the problems they cause.

A traffic jam in Bangkok, Thailand. Some governments are trying new ways to reduce the levels of pollution caused by road traffic (see right).

TRAFFIC JAMS

Many workers all over the world spend hours every month stuck in traffic jams. Even when cars are not moving, the engines use fuel and create pollution. To reduce unnecessary pollution, traffic experts recommend that drivers should turn their engines off if they do not move for more than two minutes. Some new types of car engine do this automatically!

WORKING FROM HOME

Today, more and more people in the developed world have an opportunity to work from home. By using computers and the Internet they can communicate with people around the world. Some people never have to go into an office at all. Working from home saves travel time and money, and brings pollution levels down because it reduces the number of journeys made each day.

Action stations

Unfortunately, many people have no alternative but to drive to work. To meet new environmental laws, governments have come up with schemes to help reduce the pollution and congestion these journeys cause. One simple way is for people to travel to work together. Cities in the USA have introduced car-sharing lanes on many roads — there are now 125 schemes in 30 states. These lanes are only open to cars with two or more people in them and are monitored by special traffic cameras. Car-sharing lanes are nearly always less busy than other lanes, so people using them benefit from shorter journey times.

Car-sharing lanes on motorways, such as this one, could encourage people to travel together.

Public transport

For most people, the main alternative to travelling by car is public transport. Buses, trams and trains offer a wide range of services over long and short distances. These forms of transport do less damage to the environment than cars and are safer, too.

BUSES

For many people, buses are the most convenient way to travel. They produce far less pollution than cars, even though they have bigger engines. This is because each bus can carry the same number of passengers as would fill several cars. Some cities have introduced gas-powered buses which produce even fewer emissions (see page 23).

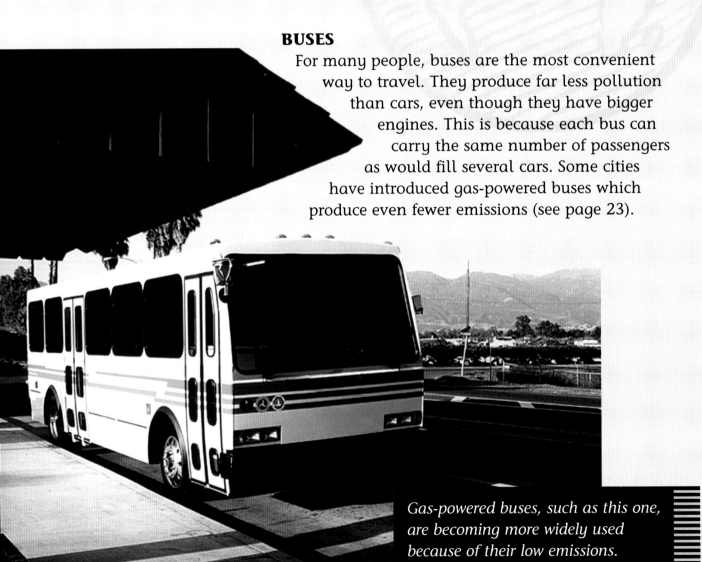

Gas-powered buses, such as this one, are becoming more widely used because of their low emissions.

TRAINS AND TRAMS

Trains are one of the most environmentally friendly or 'green' forms of transport. An average train can carry as many as 1,000 passengers at a time, using the power from a single engine. Some trains are powered by electricity, making them even greener. Trams operate in urban areas and are usually powered by electricity. They have fewer carriages and travel over shorter distances than trains.

A tram in Strasbourg, France. Trams are ideal for travelling around a busy city.

Action stations

Some governments in countries with busy cities have found ways to encourage people out of their cars and onto public transport. Drivers in Singapore, Melbourne and London have to pay a toll or charge if they want to use particular roads in the city centre. People on public transport do not have to pay the charge. These schemes have reduced the number of vehicles on the roads in these cities by around 15%.

Entering the congestion charge zone in London. Schemes such as this reduce the number of vehicles on the road, and encourage people to use public transport.

Taking to the skies

As air travel becomes more affordable, larger numbers of people are choosing to fly between cities or to travel abroad. The global increase in air traffic is having a major impact on the environment, as aeroplanes use massive amounts of fuel.

Huge aeroplane engines such as this use vast amounts of fuel.

FLYING GAS GUZZLERS

For each kilometre travelled, a large aeroplane uses more fuel than 300 cars. These aeroplanes travel thousands of kilometres every few hours and have fuel tanks that carry 150 tonnes at a time. As this fuel is burned, it produces huge amounts of carbon dioxide and other greenhouse gases. These are released into the upper atmosphere.

Aeroplanes fly thousands of kilometres and need to be refuelled regularly. They are major contributors to high carbon dioxide levels in the atmosphere.

WINGS OF CHANGE

Modern aeroplanes are not very fuel efficient. Engineers dream of aircraft that will fly much faster and use a lot less fuel. One idea being considered is for specially designed aeroplanes to fly just outside the Earth's atmosphere – in space. These would be propelled using liquid hydrogen and only produce harmless water vapour emissions.

Action stations

Aeroplane manufacturers are reducing the damage that their aeroplanes do to the environment. For example, since the 1970s Airbus has reduced the fuel consumption of its planes by 40%. In 2004, officials at Airbus met with other companies and environmental experts at the Committee on Aviation Environmental Protection (CAEP) in Montreal, Canada. The CAEP is constantly working to meet new environmental laws, such as those controlling aeroplane noise and emission levels.

These aeroplanes are manufactured by Airbus. Although they use a lot of fuel, their fuel efficiency is slowly being improved.

On the water

In some parts of the world, people regularly travel by water. In coastal cities ferries provide connections between islands and the mainland. Boats are also used to transport people along rivers, while ocean-going ships carry passengers to other countries.

ALL AT SEA

Ocean-going vessels, including ferries and cruise ships, can transport large numbers of passengers. But because of their large engines, they burn a lot of fuel and emit large quantities of greenhouse gases. To help reduce these, many new ships are fitted with special combined gas and steam turbine electric engines. These are more fuel efficient and produce fewer emissions, making them better for the environment.

This ferry is one of many that carries commuters and tourists in and out of Sydney's Circular Quay in Australia.

This hydrofoil on the Yangtze River in China is faster and uses less fuel than a conventional boat design.

ABOVE IT ALL

Some types of boat hardly touch the water at all. This lowers the amount of fuel needed to move the boat forward and so reduces the amount of fossil fuel burned. Hydrofoils have underwater 'wings' attached to legs on their hulls. These wings lift the boat up out of the water when it is moving. Catamarans have two narrow hulls which move easily through the water.

Action stations

Not all boats use engines. Sailing boats, for example, harness wind power to push them along. In Japan, the Greenheart Project is promoting the use of sail power to transport food aid and fairly-traded goods around the world (see www.greenheartproject.org). Their new, environmentally friendly small sail and solar-powered boat design does not use fuel so it has an unlimited range. It can also carry larger loads than a motorised boat of a similar size because space is not taken up by an engine.

This is an illustration of the Greenheart Project boat which could be used to transport goods. It has masts for the sails and a solar array to capture energy from the Sun.

Transporting goods

Vehicles are not just used to move people around, they are also used to move goods. Almost everything we buy has been transported to the shops from somewhere else. It may be produced nearby but very often it is brought in from far away.

IMPORTED GOODS

Some goods are brought in, or imported, from other countries. These goods are transported by road, air, rail and sea. Transporting goods over long distances in lorries or aeroplanes uses large amounts of fossil fuel and creates lots of environmental pollution. More companies are being encouraged to use rail and sea transport.

A train is perfect for transporting goods over a long distance. Most trains can move the same weight of goods as around thirty lorries.

Food is transported to supermarkets from all over the world. Look out for the labels on the fresh food shelves.

Action stations

Whenever possible, it is best to buy locally produced fruit and vegetables that have not been transported over long distances. This also applies to dairy products, such as butter and cheese. These have to be kept cold when being transported, which also uses a lot of energy.

ACCESSIBLE RAIL

Some environmental groups have joined forces with governments to reduce pollution. They aim to reduce the number of large container lorries on roads by making rail transport more accessible and affordable to companies that produce or buy goods. Lorries will always be needed for journeys between stations and shops, but hopefully in the future they will make fewer long trips.

Unfortunately, most of the containers at this port will be collected by lorries.

Fuel efficiency

Virtually all vehicles on the road today are powered by petrol or diesel. However, some of them use much more fuel than others. Fuel efficiency can be improved to reduce the amount of fuel used by vehicles. This makes them more environmentally friendly because fewer emissions are produced.

Testing a solar-powered car in a wind tunnel. These cars must be as aerodynamic as possible. The same technology can be used to improve the shape of normal cars.

IMPROVING AERODYNAMICS

One way of improving fuel efficiency is to make a vehicle more aerodynamic. Cars with smooth lines and rounded edges cut through the air more easily as they travel, so they need less fuel to move them along. This is not only better for the environment but also saves the owner money.

SMALL IS BEAUTIFUL

In general small cars use less fuel than larger cars. This is because the cars are lighter and can achieve similar speeds using smaller engines. Many governments set lower tax levels for small cars to encourage people to buy them instead of larger ones.

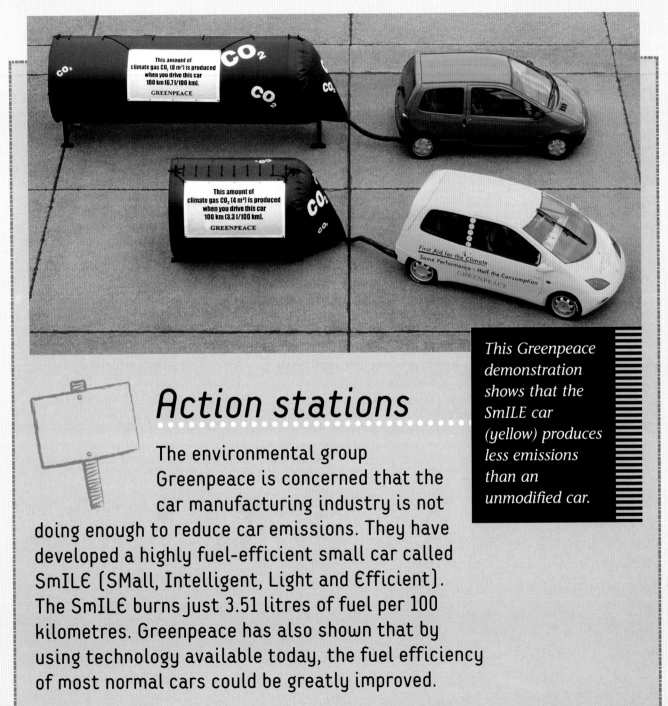

This amount of climate gas CO₂ (8 m³) is produced when you drive this car 100 km (6,7 l/100 km).
GREENPEACE

This amount of climate gas CO₂ (4 m³) is produced when you drive this car 100 km (3,3 l/100 km).
GREENPEACE

First Aid for the Climate
Same Performance - Half the Consumption
GREENPEACE

This Greenpeace demonstration shows that the SmILE car (yellow) produces less emissions than an unmodified car.

Action stations

The environmental group Greenpeace is concerned that the car manufacturing industry is not doing enough to reduce car emissions. They have developed a highly fuel-efficient small car called SmILE (SMall, Intelligent, Light and Efficient). The SmILE burns just 3.51 litres of fuel per 100 kilometres. Greenpeace has also shown that by using technology available today, the fuel efficiency of most normal cars could be greatly improved.

Cleaner fuel

A lot has been done to reduce pollution caused by burning fossil fuels in vehicle engines. But many environmental groups would like the use of fossil fuels stopped completely. More is now being done to develop 'cleaner' alternative fuels.

Many cars now run on cleaner alternative fuels, such as LPG (see right).

CUTTING EMISSIONS

Almost all petrol is now unleaded because lead was shown to cause health problems. New, low sulphur fuels are being introduced to reduce environmental damage, such as that caused by acid rain. Catalytic converters (cats) break down some chemicals in car emissions and are fitted to all new cars. Unfortunately, they do not reduce the levels of carbon dioxide.

Car emissions have been cut with changes in fuel, but more still needs to be done.

ALTERNATIVE OPTIONS

There are cleaner alternative fuels to petrol and diesel. One is liquefied petroleum gas (LPG), which is already being used to power buses in many parts of the world. Another is liquid hydrogen, thought by many scientists to be the perfect replacement for petrol. When hydrogen is burned, the main emission is water vapour, which is completely harmless.

Action stations

Biofuels, such as methanol and ethanol, are environmentally friendly fuels made from plant products, including vegetable oils. They are being used increasingly around the world because they are a source of renewable energy. Biofuel emissions are also less harmful than those produced by burning fossil fuels. Burning biofuels does produce carbon dioxide, but the crops used to generate them take in carbon dioxide as they grow. This helps carbon dioxide levels in the atmosphere to remain balanced.

This tractor in Texas, USA, is harvesting switchgrass which will be used to produce biofuel.

Electric power

Some manufacturing companies are looking at other ways to solve the problem of vehicle emissions. One solution is to power vehicles by electric motors. These produce almost no pollution at all – especially if the electricity is generated by a renewable source.

RUNNING ON ELECTRICITY

Most electric motors are powered by electricity stored in batteries, or electricity that runs along a rail or a power cable. They are used in electric trains and trams and can be found in countries all over the world. Electrically-powered cars are less common, but more are being developed. For example, in India a company called Reva has developed a car powered by batteries that can be recharged from any household power socket.

Electricity can be used to power a wide range of vehicles. However, most, such as this bus, rely on being able to recharge their batteries.

HYBRID ENGINES

Although electrically-powered cars have improved, they can only travel short distances and are slower than traditional cars. New, hybrid engines use petrol and battery power. They are more fuel efficient and produce much lower greenhouse gas emissions than traditional cars. Honda and Toyota both make hybrid electric vehicles, and other companies, including General Motors, plan to introduce them in the near future.

This engineer is producing parts for a new engine. Improvements in technology have helped to develop affordable hybrid engines.

Action stations

There are a few places where electric vehicles are more common than petrol-driven ones, and some where they are the only vehicles. On several small islands around the world, electric golf carts are the main form of transport. Although they are small and slow, they are ideal for short journeys. On Hong Kong's Lantau Island, for example, electric carts carry people through the small town of Discovery Bay. They also transport tourists and local people around the island of Caye Caulker, off the coast of Belize.

This golf cart on Caye Caulker is perfect for carrying small loads around the island, and does not produce any emissions.

Solar and magnetic power

Solar and magnetically-powered vehicles are driven by electricity and many designs are being tested. The technology is still expensive but many people believe these could be transport solutions of the future.

HARNESSING THE SUN

Solar-powered vehicles use electricity that is generated by sunlight to drive electric motors. Although they only work during the day, some solar-powered cars can run at 80 kph using the same amount of energy as it takes to power a hair dryer. A solar-powered aeroplane developed by NASA holds the world record for flying higher than any other non-rocket-powered aircraft, at 29,524 metres.

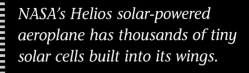
NASA's Helios solar-powered aeroplane has thousands of tiny solar cells built into its wings.

FLOATING ON AIR

Magnetically-powered vehicles use electricity to generate powerful magnetic fields, which drive them along. Magnetic levitation (maglev) trains can reach speeds of 500 kph in almost complete silence. These trains do not produce any polluting emissions because they move without an engine.

Action stations

The first maglev train went into service in January 2004 when China officially opened its first maglev train line. The line links Pudong Airport to the city of Shanghai, 30 kilometres away. The new train transports passengers into the city in just over seven minutes — a fraction of the time it used to take by taxi or traditional train. If the new line turns out to be problem free and enough money can be found, the Chinese government plans to build another maglev link, this time between Shanghai and the capital city, Beijing.

At the moment maglev trains are very expensive to build and run, but it is hoped that costs will come down in the future.

Travelling into the future

Transport makes up such a large part of our lives that scientists and engineers are constantly trying to improve it. New transport solutions must balance people's needs with environmental issues.

DRIVING CONCERNS

One of the biggest problems facing the developed world is the increasing number of cars on the roads. Instead of building new roads to reduce this congestion, environmental groups believe governments should invest more money in efficient public transport to encourage people to stop using their cars.

Anti-road protests, such as this, are becoming increasingly common in the developed world. Many environmental campaigners argue that building more roads does not help to reduce traffic congestion or pollution.

Action stations

The Segway is a new form of personal transport. It is capable of transporting one person over short distances in towns where it may help reduce traffic pollution in the future. It has two wheels and is powered by battery-driven electric motors. The Segway may not solve the world's transport problems, but it does suggest how future vehicles may look. It also shows that transport solutions can be developed with the environment in mind.

The Segway is just one idea that may reduce traffic pollution in towns and cities in the future.

INVESTING IN THE FUTURE

Affordable transport solutions are needed in the developing world to reduce poverty and improve people's lives. One source of investment, the World Bank, has already assisted many countries by providing loans – although these must be paid back. In Brazil, the railways were improved through the Brazil Railways Project and now generate money that can be reinvested in the network.

Transport networks, such as this railway in Brazil, need to be developed with people and the environment in mind.

Glossary

Acid rain Formed when sulphur dioxide and nitrogen oxides react in the atmosphere. Acid rain can make lakes acidic, poison animals and plants and even damage buildings.

Aerodynamic Shaped in a way to make movement through air easier.

Atmosphere The layer of air that surrounds the Earth.

Biofuels Liquid fuels, including ethanol, converted from organic materials.

Carbon dioxide The major greenhouse gas. Carbon dioxide is produced when fossil fuels are burned.

Catalytic converter (cat) A device fitted to a car that turns harmful exhaust gases into less toxic emissions.

Developed world The wealthier countries of the world, in which there are highly developed industries.

Developing world The poorer countries of the world, which rely more on farming than industry.

Diesel A type of liquid fossil fuel, used to power some engines.

Efficiency A measure of how much energy a machine uses as it does its job. An efficient machine uses less energy than an inefficient machine.

Emissions Waste gases, such as carbon dioxide, and tiny particles of solids that are discharged by vehicle engines.

Fossil fuels Fuels such as coal, gas or oil made from the fossilised remains of plants and animals that lived millions of years ago. Burning fossil fuels produces the greenhouse gas carbon dioxide.

Global warming The gradual rise in the Earth's temperature.

Greenhouse effect The effect of various 'greenhouse' gases in the Earth's atmosphere that trap the heat of the Sun. Many greenhouse gases are made by human activities. Their increased production is thought to be raising global temperatures.

Greenhouse gases The gases that cause the greenhouse effect. The main ones are carbon dioxide, methane and CFCs.

ITDG (Intermediate Technology Development Group) An organisation founded in 1966 by Dr E.F. Schumacher that works with local people to help find practical answers to poverty.

Lead A toxic metal produced by cars that do not run on unleaded petrol. High amounts of lead in the air are dangerous.

Pollute To release harmful substances into the environment.

Renewable energy Energy supplies, such as wind energy and solar energy, that will never be used up. They cause little or no environmental damage.

Solar To do with the Sun.

Sulphur dioxide A gas mostly produced when coal or oil is burnt in power stations. It reacts in the atmosphere to form acid rain.

Tax Money that has to be paid to the government when something is bought or used.

World Bank An international organisation which provides loans for development projects around the world.

Find out more

www.foe.co.uk/campaigns/transport
This page on the Friends of the Earth website has links to lots of excellent information on transport solutions.

www.greenhouse.gov.au
The website of the Australian government's official Greenhouse Office, this is packed with facts about global warming and the greenhouse effect.

www.itdg.org
This site provides practical answers to poverty. To find out more about transport solutions, click on the button marked 'Transport'.

www.segway.com
Discover more about this remarkable new form of transport and read stories written by people who own one.

www.eere.energy.gov/cleancities/ afdc/altfuel/altfuels.html
The website for the US-based Alternative Fuels Data Center, this is full of information on alternative fuels and the vehicles that use them.

www.hybridcars.com
This website compares all the hybrid cars currently on the market and includes a section on how hybrid engine technology works.

www.howstuffworks.com/maglev-train.htm
With the first maglev train now in operation, this explains the technology that makes it work.

Index